FORGET THE LAW

a supplemental guide to understanding business contracts

The Childress Group, LLC

Signature

Understanding Business Contracts

Supplemental Workbook

This supplemental guide includes information you will need to properly understand, draft, review, and/or negotiate your personal commercial lease agreement, non-disclosure agreement, and employment agreement. The guide includes full length contracts to guide you in learning and retention. This guide helps to further your understanding of contract terms for personal use, but does not certify or license you to provide legal or business services or give legal advice to others.

Yaminah Childress, J.D.

Published by Childress Group, LLC

Author: Yaminah Childress, J.D.

http://childressgrpllc.com

(678)884-5283

Published in the United States of America

The information provided in this publication is for educational purposes only, and does not necessarily reflect all laws, rules, or regulations for all states or territories. This publication is designed to provide accurate information concerning the subject matter covered, but it is sold with the understanding that the publisher is not offering legal advise in connection with this workbook or training. If legal services or other expert assistance is required, you may secure additional services we offer or contact another competent professional.

About Us

Childress Group, LLC provides entrepreneurs and small businesses around the world with the business development tools and services they need to succeed. Our services include virtual management services (including marketing, professional assistance, and business development), legal support services (including contract services, business formation, mediation, arbitration, and tax representation), finance services (including tax preparation and accounting) and training services (including contracts, tax planning, and starting a business). Our commitment to exceptional service, personalized care, and high quality professionalism is second to none.

The author of this book, Yaminah Childress, J.D. is the founder and CEO of Childress Group, LLC. Ms. Childress has over 15 years of combined experience in legal support, contract drafting, tax representation and preparation, and teaching. Ms. Childress has a vast expertise in business development from formation to success. Ensuring small business owners are knowledgable in their areas of interest is her top priority.

Introduction

Thank you for choosing our Understanding Business Contracts Workbook. This book, along with our live or virtual training will provide you with everything you need to draft and understand basic business contracts. We designed our course to save you time, utilizing the experience of legal professionals. It provides the essential material you need to easily grasp and retain information. This book is purposely small to ensure you don't get overwhelmed by unnecessary legal jargon.

Exclusive Offer for Owners of the Understanding Business Contracts Workbook

To receive a discount on a live or virtual training workshop to ensure your understanding of the materials, please send us one of the following documents:

- Your proof or purchase for this book, or

- Your registration confirmation for another Forget The Lawyer Training

Send by email to: info@childressgrpllc.com

Table of Contents

THIS PAGE

INTENTIONALLY

LEFT BLANK

HOW TO USE THIS WORKBOOK

This workbook was designed as a supplemental reading material with the Forget The Lawyer: Understanding Business Contracts workshop. However, it is written so that a novice reader may understand it as well, with plain language and helpful hints. The workbook provides **key terms**, **definitions**, **hypothetical examples**, **full-length contracts** with **tips, and quizzes** to ensure that you absorb the information. Please pay close attention to the following items as you proceed through this book:

Key Terms

Key terms will be highlighted throughout the book in **BOLD LETTERS**. Key terms are words that may not be common knowledge if you don't have a legal background, or work with contracts on a regular basis. All key terms have formal definitions included at the end of this workbook. Anytime you see a key term take a moment to review the definition. This ensures that you are not misunderstanding the information presented, as legal terms in many cases, has different meanings than traditional terms.

Definitions

Throughout the book, you will see italicized, text included in *(parenthesis)*. The texts within the parenthetical are key definitions summarized in layman terms. Definitions are embedded within the entire workbook to ensure your understanding of the materials presented.

Hypothetical Examples

Each section of this workbook starts with a short story that will give you an example of why you will need each particular contract, and how it relates to your business needs. Some sections allow you to provide your own examples. Actively writing, or visualizing your needs helps to promote retention.

Tips

Throughout this workbook you will come across **#Tips**. Tips are included to help you understand what you need to look out for in real life situations. Tips help you understand how an issue can arise when drafting or reviewing a contract, and how to properly address the situation.

Stop Signs

There are sections throughout the workbook that have a stop sign included. Each time you come across a stop sign, please stop! These points are critical for your assessment and retention of the materials. Think about the situation presented, how it relates to your business, and how you would address any areas of concern.

Contracts

The contracts within the book are full-length contracts that I have drafted or reviewed on behalf of other businesses. The names, dates, and details were changed or removed for confidentiality. The contracts include all of the basic legal information to ensure they are legally binding. While these contracts contain common sections and language, your contract needs may vary. For example, the commercial lease agreement included in this book contains information relevant to the business owner it was offered to. However, you may be presented with a shorter, longer, or different version of a lease agreement or any contract, as contracts are drafted based on specific business needs. Please keep in mind that the contracts within this workbook are designed to give you the tools you need to draft your own, or to be able to read and understand one being presented to you. However, if at anytime you are presented with a contract and you do not comprehend all of the information included, I advise you to hire an attorney or other contract professional that can assist you.

Quizzes

At the end of each contract you will be presented with three questions or mini hypos to test your understanding of what you just read. Your goal is to score 100% as with contracts, there are usually no second chances once you have signed on the dotted line. If you do not score 100%, please take note of what you need to review.

Section I

Forming a Valid Contract

FORMING A VALID CONTRACT

In order to get a solid understanding of any business contract or agreement, you must first understand the basics of contract formation. Contrary to what many believe, a contract does not have to be in writing in order to be legally **BINDING**. While a written agreement, signed by the **PARTY** to be charged, is surely the most effective way to ensure a contract is valid, it is not the only way. Consider oral, and other nonverbal contracts.

A binding contract "simply" needs to satisfy the following three requirements. I quote simply because, although there are only three requirements, without careful planning you could as easily complicate the process. Forming a valid contract requires the following:

1. OFFER

2. ACCEPTANCE

3. CONSIDERATION

This course starts by giving you a brief explanation of each requirement of contract formation. Remember this step is only introduced to ensure you have a basic understanding of what it means in the legal community when discussing the formation of contracts.

THE OFFER

The first step in creating a contract is offering to another, the power of creating a contractual relationship. In other words, an offer is an outward expression of your willingness to do or give something.

Example: Shania asks if you would like to become partners in a new and exciting business venture. **STOP** At that moment, an offer has been made.

Take a moment to write down an example of an offer.

_____

_____

_____

_____

_____

Accepting

The second and relatively most important step in contract formation is the acceptance requirement. An acceptance is an outward acknowledgement that the offer is established, and the parties agree to be bound by a legal relationship.

Example: The business that Shania had so excitedly offered you a partnership, sounds so amazing that you anxiously agree, and you two shake hands in affirmation. You then immediately reduce the details of your new partnership to writing. STOP At that moment, you have accepted an offer.

Take a moment to write down an example of an acceptance.

_____

_____

_____

_____

Before we move on, understand that an acceptance can be made through a writing. For instance you and Shania signed a partnership agreement detailing your new business venture, duties, and pay. However, a written agreement is not necessary to make your acceptance valid. As previously stated, a contract can be formed by oral agreement and non-verbal actions. Let's look at the example again, this time negating the writing.

Hypo: The business idea that Shania had so excitedly offered you a partnership, sounds so amazing that you anxiously agree, and you two shake hands in affirmation.

As you can see in this example, nothing was reduced to writing but, an acceptance has still occurred. The acceptance took place when you orally agreed to be a partner and you two shook hands. It is important to remember that you can form a contract by the things you say and do. Therefore, in any business dealing it is important to read things, research, and thoroughly consider all of your options before making any agreements either written, orally, or non-verbally.

Rejecting

In many cases, although an offer has been made it does not conclude in a valid contract because the offer has not been accepted. There are generally two ways to reject an offer.

1. Out right rejection: This is the simplest way to ensure a person does not think that you are accepting an offer. Say no! Yes, it's that easy. There can be no contract, if one party does not agree with the offer. However, some business owners don't want to say 'No' because they are

afraid that they may lose a good opportunity. In this case, there is another method of rejecting an offer without losing a deal, this is called a counteroffer.

2. Counteroffer: A counter offer is the simultaneous rejection of an original offer along with a new offer. A counteroffer can be made to change the terms of a contract such as cost, performance requirements, time commitments, etc. A counteroffer gives you leverage by telling the other party that you are interested in their offer, but cannot commit to the exact requirements. **An important note to remember is that a counteroffer is a rejection of an offer, and no contract has been formed unless and until the counteroffer has been accepted!** You can see that even with a counteroffer (new offer) that an acceptance must still occur.

Hypo: Instead of you immediately agreeing to Shania's partnership offer, you think for a moment and determine that you don't have the $40k capital she requires. You know the business can be a lucrative one so you decide you don't want to simply say no and walk away. So instead, you tell her you need a few days to think about the offer and get back to her. After weighing all of your options, you determine that you can come up with $25k, and make up the remaining $15k by managing the project without pay. You call Shania, and offer her the $25k and 6 months of management without pay. STOP You have just rejected Shania's offer and submitted a new offer or counteroffer.

Take a moment to write down an example of a rejection.

_____

_____

_____

_____

_____

Now that you know what it takes to form a contract, it is important to know that alongside an offer and acceptance there must be consideration.

CONSIDERATION

While a contract is deemed valid upon an offer and acceptance of that offer, the law has trouble enforcing contracts that have no consideration. What is consideration? Consideration is something of value. Keep in mind that value does not have to be significant, it can actually be one penny. Consideration is what you and the other party get in return for promising to do something or a promise to refrain from doing something.

Hypo: During partnership discussions, you and Shania agree to advance half the starting **CAPITAL**. In return for your advancement, you will receive half of the profits from the new tech toy that is sure to be a financial gold mine. The profits startup capital and shared profits are the considerations between you and Shania.

Why is consideration important? In short consideration is important when we ask Courts to enforce a contract, because a contract is technically a promise to do something. We don't want to be forced to do something we've carelessly promised simply because we said we would. In real world experiences people promise to do things all the time for many different reasons. Many promises are "empty" hold no merit or value. Therefore, consideration allows Courts to determine if you've made an empty valueless promise, or a promise that should lead to you being required to abide.

An article by Morris Cohen, a legal philosopher stated in part that "promises are sacred per se, that there is something inherently despicable about not keeping a promise, and that a properly organized society should not tolerate this…," [1] Keep this in mind when agreeing to business dealings of any kind. If you agree to it, follow through or there could be grave consequences.

Hypo: You and Shania have signed on the dotted line. You have invested the contractual half of the starting capital and everything is going smoothly. However, one year down the road as the tech toy is developed and is now for sale, you have not received any of the profits. The business is "booming," however your new business partner as utilizing all of the profits for personal gain. At this point the promise has been broken, contract breached; the courts will look at the enforceability of the agreement by the consideration, or in simpler terms, the value that was exchanged to support the formation of the contract.

---

[1]Farnsworth, E. A., Young, W. F., Sanger, C., Cohen, N. B., & Brooks, R. R. (2008). *Contracts Cases And Materials* (Seventh ed.). New York, NY: Thompson Reuter/Foundation Press.

Section II
Essential Contracts

ESSENTIAL BUSINESS CONTRACTS

In my experience many small business owners will utilize some very particular contracts and legal agreements at some point in the life cycle of their business. As it is usually the goal for small business owners to expand; the purchase or lease of real property, hiring of employees, or disclosure of sensitive and confidential information will arise. With the happening of these events you will need to know about lease agreements, employee agreements, and non-disclosure agreements, which we will cover in the following sections. You will also need to know general terms that you will find in most contracts, so let's get started.

LEASE AGREEMENTS

Business has been going great, profits are consistently climbing, and now you are ready to move out of your home office into a nice and new office or retail space. You're not quite ready to commit to a purchase of a building or other **REAL PROPERTY**, but you are ready to rent or **LEASE** a space. After viewing your potential office suite, with the large window overlooking the city, you're prepared to sign on the dotted line. **STOP** Before, you sign you need to read the

likely long, and intimidating commercial lease agreement. Without an attorney or your own knowledge, you could potentially sign yourself and your business into an agreement you didn't bargain for. And, with a signed lease agreement, it may be hard to prove to the Courts that it was not a binding agreement, considering the property owner has made an offer to rent an office suite, you accepted the offer by signing the rental agreement, and the contract was for valid consideration (office suite in lieu of a rental payment).

What is a commercial lease: A commercial lease is a contractual agreement between a property owner and business for the rental of building space (commercial property). Let's go through the details of a commercial lease agreement.

Commercial Lease

THIS LEASE is entered into as of this _____ day of January 2015, between **SAMIA INC**, a Georgia corporation (hereinafter called "Lessor") and **SARAI LLC**, a Georgia corporation (hereinafter called "Lessee").

1.   <u>DESCRIPTION OF PREMISES</u>: *(Premises: in real estate, land and the improvements on it, a building, store, shop, apartment, or other designated structure.)*

Lessor hereby leases to Lessee, and Lessee hereby hires and takes from Lessor that certain approximate **size** square foot premises commonly known as **Complete Address** (the "Leased Premises") which Leased Premises are more particularly identified on **Exhibit "A-1" (may include exhibits to clearly defined the leased area)** attached hereto. The Leased Premises are located upon the land (herein referred to as the "**LAND**") described in **Exhibit "A-2"** attached hereto and made a part hereof. For the purposes of clarification, it is acknowledged and agreed that the Leased Premises are a portion of a building containing the Leased Premises and other premises and that the term "Leased Premises" refers to all components of such building within the area identified on **Exhibit "A-1"**.

2.   <u>TERM</u>: *(Term: Fixed, non-cancelable period for which a lease agreement is in force.)*

The term of this Lease shall be for a period of **Time Frame (months, years, etc.)** commencing February 1, 2015, (the "Commencement Date") and ending January 31, <u>2017, **(Commercial lease terms are commonly longer than one year)**</u>. The term "Lease Year" as used herein shall mean a period of twelve (12) consecutive full calendar months. The first Lease Year shall begin February 1, 2015, and shall end January 31, 2016. Each succeeding Lease Year shall commence upon the anniversary date of the Commencement Date.

3.   RENTALS: *(Costs associated with renting said property, including such things as taxes, and required insurance premiums)*

Minimum Rent:

Lessee shall pay during the term hereof (without offset, deduction or abatement of any kind unless otherwise expressly provided for herein) the amounts set forth below as minimum rent (the "Minimum Rent"). Minimum Rent is due and payable monthly in advance on or before the first (1st) day of each month.

First Lease Year Monthly Rent: $3,000 per month

Second Lease Year Monthly Rent: $3,250 per month

Additional Rent:

Lessee shall pay to Lessor as additional rent (herein referred to as the "Additional Rent") certain additional amounts as set forth below in this Section 3 (the "Expense Charges"), which is equal to the sum of:

(a)   100% of all annual real estate taxes and assessments on the Land and all improvements located upon the Land; (Many commercial leases may require you to pay real estate taxes, especially if you are renting a retail space. It is important to clarify with the property owner how much real estate taxes are assessed, and if there is an expected increase.)

(b)   100% of all sanitation charges related to the Land and all improvements located upon the Land;

(c)   100% of all insurance premiums related to the Land and all improvements located upon the Land paid for by Lessor.

The Expense Charges shall be payable on a monthly basis in advance beginning on the Commencement Date in an amount equal to 1/12 of Lessor's estimate of the annual aggregate Expense Charges for such calendar year. For each calendar year of the lease, Lessor shall estimate the Expense Charges, divide that amount by 12 and bill said amount as Additional Rent on a monthly basis. At the end of each calendar year, Lessor shall bill Lessee for any Expense Charges in excess of the amount previously paid. Lessee shall pay the bill for any shortage in the Expense Charges within thirty (30) days from the date of Lessor's billing. If at the end of the calendar year, the Expense Charges are less than the amount paid, then the overage shall be applied against the next year's Expense Charges. The Expense Charges shall be prorated for any partial calendar year during the Lease Term. The Expense Charges shall constitute "Additional Rent" for all purposes under this lease and shall be paid without offset, deduction or abatement of any kind unless otherwise expressly provided for herein. The expense charges for the first year shall be _____

4.   USE OF THE PREMISES:

The Leased Premises shall be used only for **Type of Approved Use.** Lessee agrees to comply with all applicable laws, rules, regulations and ordinances of every governmental body or agency whose authority extends to the Leased Premises, or to any business conducted upon the Leased Premises.

5.   <u>TRADE FIXTURES</u>: *(A fixture is any physical property that is permanently attached to real property, the removal of which would permanently damage the real property. Some examples of fixtures are: lighting that requires installation, desks that are bolted to the floor, wash stations at salons that are bolted down, or mirrors that are placed on the wall with something other than an easily removable attachment.)*

Lessee may install equipment, furniture and trade fixtures in and upon the Leased Premises. Lessee may remove such equipment, furniture and trade fixtures, together with any other fixtures installed by Lessee or its agents, at any time during or upon the termination of this Lease so long as Lessee is not in default under this Lease and provided Lessee repairs any damage to the Leased Premises caused by reason thereof. Upon termination of this Lease, Lessee shall surrender the Leased Premises in the condition it received it as of the Commencement Date, except for normal wear and tear, permitted alterations and casualty and condemnation damage. *(It is a common practice to not allow lessees the option to remove fixtures if a lease is in default, or if you have vacated the property without removing the fixtures and repairing any damage the fixture has caused. Always keep this is mind when installing fixtures onto leased property.)*

6.   <u>ALTERATIONS AND REPAIRS</u>: *(Always thoroughly inspect leased premises before signing the lease. Look to see if you will need to make any changes to the premises so that it can be suitable for your intended purposes, or is anything needs to be fixed before moving in. It's easier to negotiate alterations or repairs before the lease is signed.)*

Lessee has fully investigated the Lease Premises and accepts the Leased Premises as suited for the uses intended by Lessee. Lessee accepts the Premises "AS IS" without relying upon any representation, warranty or covenant by Lessor with respect to the condition thereof other than as may be expressly set forth in this Lease. Accordingly, Lessee is accepting the Premises with any existing faults including, but not limited to any mold/mildew and lead paint contamination.   Lessee may make alterations to the Leased Premises; provided, however, all alterations (i) affecting any of the mechanical or utility systems (ii) structural in nature or (iii) which might reasonably be expected to result in a reduction in the value of the Leased Premises shall require Lessor's prior written consent. All alterations shall be at the sole cost and expense of Lessee. Lessor shall cooperate in all reasonable respect with Lessee at no out-of-pocket costs to Lessor to obtain necessary building permits and approvals. In addition to the foregoing, Lessee acknowledges and agrees that Lessee shall not change the exterior appearance of the Leased Premises without Lessor's prior written consent.

7.   MAINTENANCE AND REPAIRS:

Lessee shall be responsible at its sole cost and expense for **all maintenance and repairs to the Leased Premises of every kind and nature, foreseen or unforeseen, including but not**

limited to the roof, exterior or interior walls, grease traps and related drainage systems facilities, plumbing, electrical systems, heating and air conditioning systems, water lines, toilet facilities and any other systems located on the Premises or used by Lessee in its business operations. *(Always be leery when a Lessor requires you to maintain and repair every aspect of the property under all conditions.)* At its sole expense, Lessee shall keep and maintain the Leased Premises in good working order and repair.

In addition, **Lessee shall be solely responsible for the maintenance and repair of all utility systems serving the Leased Premises which are located outside of the Leased Premises such as underground water, sewer and drainage lines.** *(Always be leery when a Lessor requires you to maintain and repair utility systems, especially underground pipes. Agreeing to repaid major utility systems can be very costly.)*

Lessor may from time to time inspect the Premises to ensure that the Leased Premises are being maintained and may demand that Lessee make any required repairs to the Leased Premises. Lessee's failure to make any repair required of Lessee hereunder within thirty (30) days from Lessor's demand for those repairs shall be a default under this Lease. Lessee shall promptly repair, at its expense, any damage to the Leased Premises occurring following the date hereof caused by bringing into the Leased Premises any property for Lessee's use, or caused by the installation, removal or maintenance of such property regardless of fault or by whom such damage may be caused. **Lessor shall have no maintenance or repair obligations whatsoever with respect to the Leased Premises or the Land.**

(Always negotiate the removal or limits to this type of **CLAUSE**, a Lessor should always have some responsibility in the upkeep of major repairs and maintenance.)

8.   TAXES:

Lessor agrees to pay, before delinquency, all real property taxes and assessments assessed against the Leased Premises. Lessee agrees to pay to Lessor as Additional Rent all amounts paid by Lessor for real property taxes and assessments, as further set forth in Section 3 of this Lease. Lessee agrees to pay, before delinquency, any and all personal property taxes and license fees which have been assessed or imposed upon Lessee's personal property, fixtures and equipment installed or located in the Leased Premises. **In addition to the foregoing, Lessee shall pay as Additional Rent any sales or use tax imposed on rents collected by Lessor under this Lease or one hundred percent (100%) of any tax on rents collected in lieu of ad valorem taxes on the Land and improvements located thereon, even though laws imposing such taxes may attempt to require Lessor to pay the same**. *(Do not sign a lease where you are responsible for taxes and fees that are the responsibility of the Lessor.)*

9.   MECHANICS LIEN: *(A Mechanics Lien is typically used by subcontractors and suppliers, and is a legal claim against property that has been remodeled or improved.)*
Lessee agrees to keep the Leased Premises free from the uncontested liens of persons who, at the request of Lessee, furnish labor or material to or for the benefit of the Leased Premises, and to bond or otherwise provide security for lien claims contested by Lessee. Lessor at any time may post and keep posted on the Leased Premises appropriate notices to protect Lessor

against the claims of persons who, at the request of Lessee, furnish labor or materials to or for the benefit of the Leased Premises. It is agreed that Lessee has no authority whatsoever to bind Lessor's title to any lien claimant.

10.   UTILITIES AND COMPLIANCE WITH LAWS:

(a)   Lessee agrees to pay, before delinquency, all charges for water, gas, electricity, and any and all other utilities and services which may be used in or upon the Leased Premises. Lessor agrees that all utilities to the Leased Premises shall be separately metered.

(b)   Lessee, at its sole cost and expense, shall promptly comply with all present and future laws, ordinances, orders, rules, regulations and requirements of all federal, state and municipal governments, courts, departments, commissions, boards and officers, any national or local Board of Fire Underwriters, or any other body exercising similar functions, foreseen and unforeseen, ordinary as well as extraordinary, which may be applicable to the Leased Premises and the streets and sidewalks adjoining the Leased Premises as a result of Lessee's use of the Leased Premises, or to the use or manner of use of the Leased Premises or the owners, Lessees or occupants. **The foregoing shall be applicable whether or not such rules necessitate structural changes or improvements, or the removal or any encroachments or projections, ornamental, structural, or otherwise, onto or over the streets adjacent to the Leased Premises, or onto or over other contiguous property.** *(Do not accept conditions where you are financially responsible for major structural changes, encroachments, or improvements that require you to pay for changes that are not directly related to the exact leased premises.)*

11.   <u>ASSIGNMENT; SUBLETTING</u>: *(An assignment of a lease is a complete transfer of the right to be the tenant under the lease. Whereas, subletting is when you the legal tenant leases all of a portion of your space to another tenant (subtenant). The subtenant must pay rent and comply with the lease terms, but you, the principal tenant remains legally responsible for the lease.)*

(a)   Lessee may not assign this Lease, or sublease all or any portion of the Leased Premises, without Lessor's prior written consent. It is understood that in the event Lessor consents to any such assignment or subletting that such assignment or sublease shall not relieve Lessee of liability under the terms of this Lease. Anything contained in this Subparagraph 11(a) to the contrary notwithstanding, Lessee may assign this Lease or sublease all of the Leased Premises to an affiliate of Lessee, without Lessor's written consent, provided that (i) Lessee is not in default under this Lease and no state of facts exists that, but for the passage of time, the giving of notice or both would constitute an event of default; (ii) the assignee of an assignment assumes in writing all of Lessee's obligations under this Lease and agrees to be bound by the terms and provisions hereof from the effective date of the assignment (including sums payable after the effective date with respect to periods prior thereto); (iii) the sublessee under a sublease acknowledges that the sublease is subject to all the provisions of this Lease and agrees not to violate any of the restrictions or prohibitions of this Lease, including but not limited to, the use clause set forth in Paragraph 4 hereof; and (iv) the assignment and assumption or sublease is evidenced by a written document, an executed copy of which is promptly delivered to Lessor. As used in the prior sentence, the term "affiliate" means a person or entity controlling, controlled by or under common control with Lessee, except for persons or entities acquiring control of Lessee as part of the process in which the assignment or sublease taken place, and partners and joint ventures of Lessee in the business being conducted on the Leased Premises. As used in this Paragraph (a), the term "control" means ownership of more than fifty percent (50%) of either the voting rights of a corporation or the rights to manage the ordinary business of a partnership.

(b)   If Lessee assigns its interest in this Lease, (i) Lessor shall give the Lessee a copy of any notice of default sent to assignee, such copy to be sent to the last notice address of the Lessee provided to Lessor and otherwise as provided in Paragraph 18, but failure to give such copy shall not prevent Lessor from exercising all remedies against assignee; (ii) Lessor shall accept the performance by the Lessee of any of assignee's obligations under this Lease as if it were performance by Lessee; (iii) Lessor shall recognize the exercise by the Lessee of any re-entry or reverter retained by the Lessee in connection with this Lease; and (iv) if Lessor terminates this Lease for a default by assignee, Lessor shall offer to lease the Leased Premises to the Lessee on the terms and conditions of this Lease for the unexpired balance of the term of this Lease at the date of its termination, on the condition that the Lessee cure all defaults by assignee and pay all sums owed Lessor as a consequence of such defaults, and the failure of Lessor to offer such lease will release the Lessee of its liability under Subparagraphs 20(b)(3)(ii) and 20(b)(3)(iii).

12.   <u>INDEMNITY AND INSURANCE</u>: *(Indemnity: The transfer of risk from one party to another.)*

(a)   Lessee agrees to indemnify and save Lessor harmless from and against any and all claims and demands arising from any act, omission, or negligence of Lessee, or its contractors, licensees, agents, servants, or employees, or arising from any accident, injury or damages whatsoever caused to any person or property occurring in, on or about the Leased Premises or any part of them, and any and all actions, suits and proceedings in connection with any such claim or demand and any and all loss, damage, expenses and liability incurred in or in connection with any such claim or demand, including attorneys' fees and court costs. *(Ensure that the Lessor agrees to indemnify you as well.)*

(b)   Lessee shall maintain in full force during the term of this Lease, a policy or policies of comprehensive liability insurance, including property damage, covering the Leased Premises and its use and occupation by Lessee, insuring against liability for injuries to persons and property and for death of any person or persons occurring in or about the Leased Premises. The liability under such insurance shall not be less than ONE MILLION AND NO/100 DOLLARS ($1,000,000.00) for property damage, not less than ONE MILLION AND NO/100 DOLLARS ($1,000,000.00) for personal injury, including death, for any one person, and not less than TWO MILLION AND NO/100 DOLLARS ($2,000,000.00) for personal injury to more than one person in any one accident *(Insurance coverage limits will be different depending on the nature of your business and value of leased premises.)* Lessee agrees to name Lessor as additional insured, to obtain an endorsement to include the contractual obligations of Lessee, including any indemnification agreement of Lessee under this Lease, and shall furnish a certificate of insurance to Lessor.

(c)   Lessee shall give Lessor notice of all claims made against the Lessee that come within the scope of the indemnification of this Section, and shall not settle any such claim without the Lessor's written consent. Unless objected to by an insurer of the Lessee that acknowledges primary responsibility for the claim, the Lessor shall be entitled, but shall not be required, to conduct the defense of the claim. In the event Lessor defends the claim, the Lessee shall cooperate with the Lessor in defending the claim, including without limitation, providing documents, witnesses and other sources of information within its reasonable control.

13.   DAMAGE OR DESTRUCTION:

(a)   If the Leased Premises or any portion thereof is damaged or destroyed by fire, flood, tornado or by the elements, or through any casualty, or otherwise, after the commencement of the Lease Term, this Lease shall continue in full force and effect, and Lessor at its expense shall (so long as insurance proceeds are available therefore) promptly restore, repair or rebuild the portions of the Leased Premises to the same condition as it existed on the Commencement Date, within 90 days after receipt of Lessor's insurance proceeds payable as a result of such damage or destruction. In the event Lessor fails to restore the Leased Premises as aforesaid, Lessee's sole remedy against Lessor shall be to terminate this Lease, as of the date of such casualty. Minimum Rent and Additional Rent, if any, shall abate from the date of such damage or destruction until ten (10) days after Lessor has repaired or restored the building in the manner and in the condition provided in this Section and notified Lessee of such fact. In the event that a part only of the Leased Premises is untenable or incapable of use for the normal conduct of Lessee's business therein, a just and proportionate part of the rent shall be **ABATED** from the date of such damage until ten (10) days after Lessor has completely repaired same and notified Lessee of such fact.

(b)   In the event that the Leased Premises shall be damaged in whole or in substantial part within the last twelve (12) months of the Term, Lessor or Lessee shall have the option, exercisable within ninety (90) days following such damage, of terminating this Lease, effective as of the date of mailing notice thereof.

(c)   No damage or destruction to the Leased Premises shall allow Lessee to surrender possession of the Leased Premises nor affect Lessee's liability for the payment of rent or any other covenant contained herein, except as specifically provided in this Lease. Notwithstanding any of the provisions herein to the contrary, Lessor shall have no obligation to rebuild the Premises unless the damage or destruction is a result of a casualty covered by Lessor's insurance policy.

(d)   Lessee shall give to Lessor prompt written notice of any damage to or destruction of any portion of the Leased Premises resulting from fire or other casualty.

(e)   Lessor shall not be liable for any damage to property of Lessee or of others located on the Leased Premises, nor for the loss of or damage to any property of Lessee or of others by theft or otherwise. Lessor shall not be liable for any injury or damage to persons or property resulting from fire, explosion, falling plaster, steam, gas, electricity, water, rain or snow or leaks from any part of the Leased Premises or from the pipes, appliances or plumbing works or from the roof, street or subsurface or from any other place or by dampness or by an other cause of whatsoever nature. *(It is a best practice if you include the following or similar terms; "except for any negligence act or omission caused by Lessor".)* Lessor shall not be liable for any such damage caused by other Lessees or persons in the Leased Premises, occupants of property adjacent to the Leased Premises, or the public, or for damage caused by operations in construction of any private, public or quasi-public work. Lessor shall not be liable for any defect in the Leased Premises. All property of Lessee kept or stored on the Leased Premises shall be so kept or stored at the risk of Lessee only, and Lessee shall hold Lessor harmless from any claim arising out of damage to the same, including **SUBROGATION** claims by Lessee's insurance carriers.

14. INSPECTION:

Lessor may enter upon the Leased Premises at any reasonable time for the purpose of inspecting the Leased Premises. Lessor shall be permitted to show the Leased Premises to prospective purchasers at any time and to prospective lessees within six (6) months prior to expiration of this Lease.

15. BANKRUPTCY:

If the then Lessee shall become insolvent or make an assignment for the benefit of creditors, or file a petition in bankruptcy or seek the benefit of any bankruptcy composition or insolvency law or act, or if the then Lessee shall be adjudged bankrupt, or if a receiver or trustee of the Leased Premises of the Lessee shall be appointed, or this Lease shall by operation of law devolve upon or pass to any person or persons other than the Lessee, then in each such case

Lessor shall have all rights and remedies available by law including, but not limited to the right to terminate this Lease.

16.   BINDING ON SUCCESSORS: *(Successor: A person who succeeds another. This would include a person or entity you have assigned or sublet your lease to.)*

The provisions of this Lease shall be binding upon and inure to the benefit of the permitted successors and assigns and legal representatives of the parties hereto.

17.   SHORT FORM OF LEASE:

Upon Lessor's request, Lessee agrees to execute a memorandum or short form of this Lease in recordable form and on such terms as are acceptable to Lessor and Lessee. Upon termination of this Lease, Lessor may require Lessee to execute, in recordable form, a cancellation of this Lease and the memorandum or short form thereof. Lessee hereby makes, constitutes and appoints Lessor, as its true and lawful attorney-in-fact for Lessee and in its name, place and stead to execute and record a cancellation of this Lease and the memorandum thereof. This **POWER OF ATTORNEY** is coupled with an interest and is irrevocable.18.

18.   NOTICES: *(Notice is the legal concept describing a requirement that a party be aware of legal process affecting their rights, obligations or duties.)*

(a)   All notices, requests, demands, approvals, consents and other communications authorized or required hereunder ("notices") shall be in writing. To be valid in the absence of written acknowledgment of receipt by the recipient, notice must be given by (i) registered, or certified mail, postage prepaid, return receipt requested, addressed to the recipient's notice address, (ii) prepaid courier or express mail service, telegram or mailgram, where the carrier provides or retains evidence of the date of delivery, sent to the recipient's notice address or (iii) personal service upon the recipient, if an individual, upon a general partner, if the recipient is a partnership, or upon an officer, if the recipient is a corporation.

(b)   The notice addresses of the parties are as follows:

LESSOR: *(Include complete mailing addresses in both sections.)*

LESSEE:

Either party may change the person or place in its notice address by notice given pursuant to this Paragraph. A post office box may not be used as the notice address for Lessor or Lessee.

(c)   Notice shall be deemed given when delivered to the notice address or personally served, except that (i) notice which must be given by a certain time to be valid or which is sent: registered, postage prepaid, shall be deemed given when posted, and (ii) notice which starts the running of a time period when it is given and which is delivered to the notice address on a non-business day shall be deemed given the next business day if left at the notice address, or the next business day when re-delivered to the notice address if not left at the notice address. Refusal to accept delivery or absence of anyone at a notice address to accept delivery shall not prevent notice from being given. A non-business day is Saturday, Sunday or legal holiday generally observed in the city where notice is delivered.

19.　CONDEMNATION: *(Condemnation: The process of implementing Eminent Domain, whereby the government takes private property for public use.)*

In the event of any taking or damage of all or any part of the Leased Premises, or ingress, egress, or parking in connection therewith or any interest therein by reason of any exercise of the power of eminent domain, whether by a condemnation proceeding or otherwise, or any transfer made in avoidance of an exercise of the power of eminent domain (all of the foregoing being hereafter referred to as the "appropriation") prior to or during the term hereof (or any extension or renewal thereof), the rights and obligations of Lessor and Lessee with respect to such appropriation shall be hereafter provided. In the event of an appropriation of all of the Leased Premises, except for a temporary period, this Lease shall terminate as of the date of such appropriation. In the event of an appropriation of less than all of the Leased Premises, if the appropriation shall include (i) any portion of the building located on the Leased Premises, or (ii) the access from the Leased Premises to a public road nearest to the Leased Premises, then in such event Lessor or Lessee shall each have the option to terminate this Lease. Any such election shall be made by written notice given within thirty (30) days after appropriation. Any such termination shall be effective the date the condemner takes title or possession, whichever occurs first. All compensation awarded or paid upon such a total or partial taking of the Leased Premises shall belong to and be the property of Lessor without any participation by Lessee; provided, however, that nothing contained herein shall be construed to preclude Lessee from prosecuting any claim directly against the condemning authority in such condemnation proceedings for loss of business, and/or depreciation to, damage to, and/or cost of removal of, and/or for the value of stock and/or trade fixtures, furniture and other personal property belonging to Lessee. If this Lease is not terminated, Lessor shall promptly make any restoration of the Leased Premises necessitated by reason of appropriation. In the event of appropriation of less than all of the Leased Premises, if this Lease is not terminated pursuant to this Section, the rental and other obligations of Lessee hereunder shall be abated for the remainder of the term in an equitable amount. If this Lease is terminated, the Rental and all other obligations of Lessee shall be prorated to the date of termination and Lessor shall refund to Lessee the Rental and other payments made by Lessee for any period beyond the date of termination.

Lessor shall notify Lessee in writing of any proposed condemnation of which Lessor has actual knowledge and include such information available to Lessor as shall enable Lessee to determine the property affected.

20.   Default Lessor Remedies

(a)   The occurrence of any of the following shall constitute a default by Lessee:

(i)   Failure to timely pay rent or any other monetary sum when due, and such amount remains unpaid by Lessee seven (7) days after written notice from Lessor to Lessee, provided **Lessor shall not be required to give such notice more than once in any twelve (12) month period.** *(Clauses such as this may not be valid. It is common practice that a Lessor must give written notice to a Lessee each time a rental agreement is in default for failure to pay timely rent, not just once every 12 months.)*

(ii)   Failure to perform any other provision of this Lease if the failure to perform is not cured within 30 days after written notice has been given to Lessee. If the default cannot reasonably be cured within 30 days, Lessee shall not be in default of this Lease, if Lessee commences to cure the default within the 30-day period and diligently and in good faith continues to cure the default; provided, however, that in no event shall such cure period extend beyond sixty (60) days after the date of such notice.

(iii)   The abandonment, vacating or failure to do business in the Leased Premises, or any substantial portion thereof, by the Lessee.

(iv)   Lessee is adjudicated bankrupt, or a permanent receiver is appointed for Lessee's property and such receiver is not removed within sixty (60) days after written notice from Lessor to Lessee to obtain such removal.

(v)   Lessee, either voluntarily or involuntarily, takes advantage of any debtor relief proceedings under any present or future law, whereby the rent or any part thereof is, or is proposed to be, reduced or payment thereof deferred.

(vi)   Lessee makes an assignment for the benefit of creditors.

(b)   Lessor shall have the following remedies in case of Lessee's default:

(i)   To immediately enter upon and remove all persons and property from the Leased Premises, storing said personal property in a public warehouse or elsewhere at cost of, and for the account of, Lessee. No such re-entry or taking possession of Leased Premises by Lessor shall be construed as an election on its part to terminate this Lease.(ii)   To collect by suit or otherwise each installment of rent or other sum as it becomes due hereunder, or to enforce by suit or otherwise any other term or provision hereof on the part of Lessee required to be performed.

(iii)   To terminate this Lease, in which event, this Lease shall terminate if Lessee has not cured its default prior thereto and Lessee shall surrender immediately possession of the Leased Premises, and to pay to Lessor all expenses Lessor may incur by reason of the default, including the cost of recovering the Leased Premises, and including:

(1)   The worth at the time of award of the unpaid rent which had been earned at the time of termination; and

(2)   The worth at the time of award of the amount by which the unpaid rent which would have been earned after termination until the time of award exceeds the amount of such rental loss that the Lessee proves could have reasonably been avoided; and

(3)   The worth at the time of the award of the amount by which the unpaid rent for the balance of the term after the time of award exceeds the amount of such rental loss that the Lessee proves could be reasonably avoided; and

(4)   Any other amount necessary to compensate the Lessor for all reasonable expenses of Lessor in enforcing its remedies and re-letting the Leased Premises, including the costs of non-structural alterations and renovations.

(iv)   To cure such failure by Lessee for the account and at the expense of Lessee, all payments made by Lessor in curing such failure by Lessee to be deemed additional rent under this Lease and shall become immediately due and payable. Should Lessor re-enter and not elect to terminate this Lease, it may from time to time re-let the Leased Premises or any part thereof, as the agent and for the account of Lessee, either in Lessor's name or otherwise, upon such terms and conditions and for such period (whether longer than the balance of the term hereof or not) as Lessor may deem advisable, in which even the rents received on such re-letting during the balance of the term of this Lease or any part thereof shall be applied first to the expenses of re-letting and collection (including necessary renovation and alteration of the Leased Premises and reasonable attorneys' fees and any real estate commission actually paid) and, thereafter, toward payment of all sums due or to become due to Lessor hereunder, and if such rents shall not be sufficient to pay such sums, Lessee shall pay to the Lessor monthly any deficiency.(c)　　Each and all of the remedies given to Lessor hereunder are cumulative. The exercise of one right or remedy by Lessor shall not impair its right to any other remedy. **Lessee hereby waives all claims for damages that may be caused by Lessor in re-entering and taking possession of the Leased Premises as herein provided.**

(Regardless of the situation, never relinquish all of your rights. While some damages may occur if a Lessor has to forcible re-enter property, that does not give them the legal right to intentionally or negligently damage your property.)

Lessor will dismiss with prejudice any action or proceeding to re— enter or regain possession of the Leased Premises, provided that (i) Lessee pays Lessor all amounts in default and all Lessor's expenses incurred as a result of the default, including costs and reasonable attorneys' fees in bringing the action or proceeding, and (ii) Lessee has not caused the dismissal of an action or proceeding pursuant to this provision within the previous twelve (12) months. A settlement of an action or proceeding by Lessor to re-enter or regain possession of the Leased

Premises wherein Lessee does not pay the entire amount claimed by Lessor to be due shall not be deemed a use of this provision by Lessee.

21.   QUIET ENJOYMENT: (A Covenant that promises that the Lessor or Lessee of an estate in real property will be able to possess the premises in peace, without disturbance by hostile claimants.)

Lessor warrants, represents and covenants that it is the owner of the property leased herein and covenants and agrees that, provided Lessee complies with each and all of the terms of this Lease, Lessor shall defend Lessee's right of quiet possession against all parties claiming by, through or under Lessee.

22.   WRITTEN CONSENT:

Whenever the "prior written consent" or "prior written approval" of either Lessor or Lessee is referred to in this Lease, it is understood and agreed that except as might otherwise be provided for herein to the contrary, such consent shall not be unreasonably withheld, conditioned or delayed by Lessor or Lessee, and if withheld, the reason therefore shall be stated in writing. If the party whose consent or approval is required does not deny such consent or approval in a written notice stating the reason for such denial within thirty (30) days from the date of the request for such consent or approval, such consent or approval shall be deemed to have been given.

23.   LATE CHARGE:

If Lessor fails to receive any rent within **specified number of days** after it becomes due, then Lessee shall be obligated to pay Lessor a late fee of **specified fixed rate or percentage** of the overdue amount of rent (not including interest). In addition, in the event any amount remains unpaid for a period of ten (10) days after the date it becomes due, then Lessee shall be obligated to pay interest on such amount from that date which is the 30th day following the date such payment was originally due until paid, at a rate of eighteen (18%) percent per year, or, if less, at the maximum rate of interest permitted by law. The parties agree that such late charges do not constitute a penalty, but rather represent a fair and reasonable estimate of the costs Lessor will incur by reason of such late payment. The assessment of such charges shall not relieve Lessee of its obligation to pay rent on a timely basis.

24.   ESTOPPEL CERTIFICATE: *(Estoppel is defined as a legal principle that stops someone from asserting a truth that is defined as contradictory to an already established truth.)*

(d)   Lessor and Lessee shall at any time upon not less than **specified days** prior written notice from the other execute and deliver to the other a statement in writing identifying the signatory as the current Lessor or Lessee under this Lease and certifying as to any or all of the following matters: (i) the documents which then comprise this Lease; (ii) that this Lease is in full force and effect if such is the case; or   otherwise, if not; (iii) that there are not, to the certifying party's knowledge, any uncured defaults on the part of the other party or any acts which but for the passage of time or the giving of notice or both would constitute such a default (or specifying such default or acts, if any are claimed); (iv) the expiration date of the Lease term and the number and duration of any unexercised options to extend or renew the Lease term; (v) the then current annual amount of rent and all other periodic charges paid by Lessee and the dates through which each has been paid; (vi) in the case of Lessee, that it has no defense against the enforcement by Lessor of the terms of this Lease, (or specifying the nature of each defense); (vii) the resolution of any matter left to future determination by the terms of this Lease; (viii) any other matter relating to this Lease or the Leased Premises, that the requesting party may reasonably requires; and (ix) that the certifying party is not subject to any bankruptcy proceeding.

(e)   The statement shall be addressed only to parties who have acquired or are about to acquire an interest in all or any part of the Leased Premises (including any lender acquiring security title to the Leased Premises) from the party requesting the statement, or to a party issuing title insurance in connection with said acquisition. Only parties of the type described in the preceding sentence to whom the statement is addressed may rely conclusively upon the statements contained therein, notwithstanding that the statement may be addressed to or delivered to other parties or that the statement may contain terms or provisions to the contrary. The obligation of the party giving the statement shall be limited to the obligation not assert a position contrary to the statement against the party to whom the statement may be and is properly addressed.

25.   WAIVER OF PROPERTY DAMAGE CLAIM:

Lessor and Lessee hereby release each other from all liability for damage to the real and personal property of the releasing party located on the Leased Premises that is caused by risks insured against under fire and extended coverage insurance available at the time the loss occurs or actually in force under which the releasing party is insured. If a waiver of subrogation cannot be obtained by the releasing party from its insurer except by the payment of an additional premium amount, then the releasing party shall notify the other party and the other party shall have the option of paying the increase in premium or penalty or losing the benefit of the release.

26.   WAIVER OF RIGHTS

No failure of Lessor to exercise any power given Lessor hereunder or to insist upon strict compliance by Lessee of its obligations hereunder and no custom or practice of the parties at variance with the terms hereof shall constitute a waiver of Lessor's right to demand exact compliance with the terms hereof.

27.   SECURITY DEPOSIT.

Within **specified days** of execution hereof by Lessee, Lessee shall deposit with Lessor the sum of **Dollar amount** as a security deposit (the "Security Deposit"). The Security Deposit shall be held by Lessor as security for the faithful performance by Lessee of all of the provisions of this Lease to be performed or observed by Lessee. If Lessee fails to pay Rental or other charges due hereunder, or otherwise defaults with respect to any provision of this Lease, Lessor may use, apply or retain all or any portion of the Security Deposit for the payment of any Rental or other charge in default or for the payment of any other sum to which Lessor may become obligated by reason of Lessee's default, **or to compensate Lessor for any loss or damage which Lessor may suffer thereby.**

(Security deposits should not be used as compensation. Instead Lessors are usually allowed to use all or a portion of the security deposit to cover damages, and in some cases past due rent.) Such use, application or retention of the Security Deposit shall not prohibit or limit Lessor's exercise of any other remedies Lessor may have for Lessee's default. The Security Deposit, or so much thereof as has not theretofore been applied by Lessor, shall be returned, without payment of interest or other increment for its use, to Lessee (or, at Lessor's option, to the last assignee, if any, of Lessee's interest hereunder) upon the later to occur of (i) the expiration date of the Lease or (ii) the date on which Lessee has performed all of Lessee's obligations under this Lease.

28.   MISCELLANEOUS:

TIME IS OF THE ESSENCE with respect to this Lease. This Lease, including any exhibits hereto, constitutes the entire agreement between the parties hereto, and there are no other agreements or understandings, either oral or written, between them concerning the subject matter of this Lease other than those herein set forth. No amendment, change, waiver or modification to this Lease shall be binding upon the parties hereto, unless in writing and signed by the parties hereto. If any provision hereof is for any reason unenforceable or inapplicable, the other provisions hereof will remain in full force and effect in the same manner as if such unenforceable or inapplicable provision had never been contained herein. *(Most contracts include a clause that acknowledges unenforceable provisions. While there may be sections, statements, or words in a contract that are deemed unenforceable, these clauses act as a provision to ensure that the entire contract is not invalidated.)* The parties acknowledge that each party and its counsel have reviewed and approved this Lease and that the normal rule of construction to the effect that any ambiguities are to be resolved against the drafting party shall not be employed in the interpretation of this Lease or any amendments or exhibits hereto. Without regard to principles of conflicts of laws, the validity, interpretation, performance and enforcement of this Lease shall be governed by and construed in accordance with the laws of the **State of** _____.

[Signature and date section omitted]

By looking at this lease agreement you should have discovered some words and provisions that are similar to those of a residential lease agreement, had you ever encountered one. However, keep in mind that commercial lease agreements are usually more extensive and stricter than residential agreements. With that stated, don't be intimidated by the length. With this example, you should be able to compare this lease to any lease agreement, and have an idea of what is being outlined, what is valid, what should be invalid, and give you adequate room to negotiate. The key to getting a lease agreement with terms beneficial to both parties, is the understanding of key terms, and the willingness and confidence to negotiate on your own behalf.

#**Tip:** Remember that even some Lessors are small business owners and just starting out. Drafting, understanding and/or negotiating lease agreements may not be their strongest skill set either.

#**Tip:** Never sign a lease agreement or any contract without giving yourself adequate time to read and absorb the language. It is ok for you to request a copy to take home and read through in its entirety before committing to the terms and conditions.

Quiz 1

1. What is a Lessor?

    a. A person who rents a property

    b. The owner of real property who agrees to lease their land to another

    c. An amount less than another amount

2. If a lease agreement contains a clause stating that you are required to pay all property taxes, what are your options?

    a. Negotiate the terms of the agreement, decline, agree or counter-offer

    b. Agree to the terms as written because they are included in the full agreement, in which the rest you agree

    c. Offer to pay a portion of the property taxes or refuse to sign the contract

3. You have decided to bring a claim against the management company who leased you a commercial property. Once you get to court the Attorney for the Defendant finds that a statement with the lease agreement is unenforceable as against the management company. What does this mean for you?

    a. You will lose your claim because your contract has been found not to be legally binding

    b. You must amend your complaint because the contract is invalid

    c. Request that the court consider the remaining contract valid, as the one clause does not invalidate the entire agreement

NONDISCLOSURE AGREEMENTS

Business is doing great and you are ready to take your next step. You've thought about adding a very unique product you have pondered on for quite sometime. However, you don't have the expertise in creating the application for the product. You're stuck, you need someone who is experienced in information technology, but you don't trust anyone with your idea. What do you do? Well, if your idea has been copyrighted or patented your idea is protected, but lets assume that at this point it is not. Before you go and share your top-secret ideas with anyone who will listen, or the IT guy who may be able to help you turn your idea into something real… STOP You can utilize a contractual agreement known as a Nondisclosure Agreement to protect your sensitive business information.

What is a Non-Disclosure Agreement? A nondisclosure agreement also known as a confidentiality agreement is a contract by which one or more parties agree not to disclose confidential information that they have shared with each other as a necessary part of doing business together.

Now let's break down the essentials of a nondisclosure agreement.

Nondisclosure Agreement

1. The Parties (Parties to a contract are commonly known as the promisee and promisor. Two or more **ENTITIES** where one side will receive a contractual benefit while the other side holds the obligation to provide the benefit.)

This Nondisclosure Agreement (the "Agreement") is entered into by and between Disclosing party **(The person or business sharing the information)**, and receiving party **(The person or business receiving the confidential information)**, for the purpose of preventing the unauthorized disclosure of Confidential Information as defined below. The parties agree to enter into a confidential relationship with respect to the disclosure of certain proprietary and confidential information ("Confidential Information").

2. Definition of Confidential Information *(It is always important to define what confidential information is in general or broad terms. Try not to be too specific, as you may inadvertently leave out key details.)*

For purposes of this Agreement, "Confidential Information" shall include all information or material that has or could have commercial value or other utility in the businesses in which Disclosing Party is engaged. If Confidential Information is in written form, the Disclosing Party shall label or stamp the materials with the word "Confidential" or some similar warning. If Confidential Information is transmitted orally, the Disclosing Party shall promptly provide a writing indicating that such oral communication constituted Confidential Information. All fax, email and electronic communications are considered confidential.

3. Exclusions From Confidential Information

Receiving Party's obligations under this Agreement do not extend to information that is: (a) publicly known at the time of disclosure or subsequently becomes publicly known through no fault of the Receiving Party; (b) discovered or created by the Receiving Party before disclosure by Disclosing Party; (c) learned by the Receiving Party through legitimate means other than from the Disclosing Party or Disclosing Party's representatives; or (d) is disclosed by Receiving Party with Disclosing Party's prior written approval. *(Public information is always excluded from nondisclosure agreements. Think of it this way, if you told someone, friend, other business, etc., your confidential information and that person told the party to this contract, it is no longer confidential. If it is available through the use of a public record search, it is not confidential, if someone can do a web search on you or your company and the information is available, then it is not confidential.)*

#Tip: Do not share your confidential information with anyone if it is not for legitimate business purposes, and the receiving party has not signed a nondisclosure agreement. As soon as you make confidential information public this agreement becomes void as to the disclosed information.

4. Obligations of Receiving Party

Receiving Party shall hold and maintain the Confidential Information in strictest confidence for the sole and exclusive benefit of the Disclosing Party. Receiving Party shall carefully restrict access to Confidential Information to employees, contractors and third parties as is reasonably required and shall require those persons to sign nondisclosure restrictions at least as protective as those in this Agreement. Receiving Party shall not, without prior written approval of Disclosing Party, use for Receiving Party's own benefit either for private or commercial use, publish, copy, or otherwise disclose to others, or permit the use by others for their benefit or to the detriment of Disclosing Party, any Confidential Information including but not limited to trade secrets, business plans and financial records. Receiving Party shall return to Disclosing Party any and all records, notes, and other written, printed, or tangible materials in its possession pertaining to Confidential Information immediately if Disclosing Party requests it in writing.

5. Time Periods *(Your time period should be perpetual, meaning it should not end until you decide the information is no longer confidential.)*

The nondisclosure provisions of this Agreement shall survive the termination of this Agreement and Receiving Party's duty to hold Confidential Information in confidence shall remain in effect until the Confidential Information no longer qualifies as a trade secret or until Disclosing Party sends Receiving Party written notice releasing Receiving Party from this Agreement, whichever occurs first.

6. Relationships *(Include a relationship section. Simply making the other party aware that just because you have business dealings, does not make you business partners in any capacity.)*

Nothing contained in this Agreement shall be deemed to constitute either party a partner, joint venturer or employee of the other party for any purpose.

7. Entire Agreement *(It's important to include this clause. In the legal community there is a rule known as parole evidence. Parole evidence prevents a party from introducing evidence outside of a signed contractual agreement. This helps to ensure the Courts know you intended for this written contract to be the only contractual understanding between you and the other party.)* This is the entire agreement between the parties. It replaces and supersedes any and all oral agreements between the parties, as well as any prior writings. This Agreement may not be amended except in a writing signed by both parties.

8. Successors and Assignees

This agreement binds and benefits the heirs, successors, and assignees of the parties.

9. Waiver

The failure to exercise any right provided in this Agreement shall not be a waiver of prior or subsequent rights.

(In business it is important to follow exact procedures. For example, this agreement states that a written confidential disclaimer must follow any confidential information made orally. If you forget to send a "writing," stating that the oral information was confidential, you could void your agreement. Adding a waiver clause gives you a little "cushion". If you forget to send the written disclosure statement, you can save yourself from losing all of your rights.)

10. Governing Law

This agreement will be governed by and construed in accordance with the laws of the state of _____.

11. Severability

If any court determines that any provision of this agreement is invalid or unenforceable, any invalidity or unenforceability will affect only that provision and will not make any other provision of this agreement invalid or unenforceable and this Agreement shall be modified, amended, or limited only to the extent necessary to render it valid and enforceable.

This Agreement and each party's obligations shall be binding on the representatives, assigns, and successors of such party. Each party has signed this Agreement through himself or its authorized representative. Electronic and digitized signatures are effective as a written signature.

[Signature and date section omitted]

#Tip: Nondisclosure agreements can be used for virtually any type of business dealing, and with any business or individual you see fit. If information is important for you and your business to keep under the strictest confidence, then this agreement is essential. Some uses include: Trade secrets such as ingredients, design layouts, or blueprints; undisclosed financial information including bank account numbers and transactions; or confidential knowledge to name a few.

#Tip: A nondisclosure agreement can go both ways, and be mutually beneficial. You can protect your information, while the other party is protecting theirs.

#Tip: Remember that information can lose its confidentiality over time. Ensuring that you properly use this agreement and refrain from casually sharing information, can prolong the time in which your information remains legally confidential.

Quiz 2

1. What can be included in a non-disclosure agreement?

    a. Financial information, blueprints, trade-secrets, business plans

    b. Property address, business plan, financial information, employee roles

    c. Ingredients, trade-secrets, criminal background information

2. What is considered disclosure of information?

    a. Telling your friend in confidence

    b. Emailing information to another party including a confidential disclosure statement under your signature

    c. Writing the information down in your personal journal where you later put it in your bedroom drawer

    d. All of the above

    e. None of the above

3. You create a business plan for a start-up that you have been dreaming about for several years. The only issue you have is finding someone who can help you build a web application. You are referred to Andre who is known as an expert in his field. You ask that he sign a nondisclosure agreement because you believe your idea is new and innovative. He happily agrees and the contract is now formed. Has Andre become your business partner once he has signed the agreement?

   a. Yes

   b. No

   c. I don't know, more information is needed

The final legal contract that we will cover is an Employment Agreement. You have your new prime office location, your new product is selling off shelves, but you've discovered that your one-man team is not going to take you to the next level. It's true in business, we can't do everything alone. It's time for you to decrease your outsourced work, and hire a full-time staff. What will you need? What will they expect? How can you be certain that this employee is the person they claim to be? You can go the traditional route, solicit applications and resumes, run background checks, and motor vehicle reports, which is certainly the perfect way to start! But **STOP** before you officially hire them, and bring them into your world of finance, design ideas, business strategies, etc., you should require them to sign an employment agreement. This is especially important for top-level employees that will likely have access to your businesses most confidential information.

What is an Employment Agreement, and why is it important? An employment agreement is a contract between an employer and employee that details the employment relationship. This document is important, because it will show clearly the rate of pay, benefits, roles and responsibilities, start date, and end dates (if on a contract term). In addition, an employment agreement may include a nondisclosure clause like our previous example. It can also include a non-compete agreement, which is important if you plan to share trade secrets with your employee(s). In simple terms, this agreement is one of the most important agreements that you can have in business, because it ensures that the entire team is on the same page.

Let's take a closer look at an Employment Agreement. The sample that follows includes both a nondisclosure and non-compete clauses.

Employment Agreement

1. Identification of Employer and Employee

This agreement (the "Agreement") is entered into by and between employer and disclosing party name **(Include legal business name and complete address)** and Employee herein referred to as Employee and Receiving party name **(Employee or contractors name and address)**.

2. Employment Status

In consideration of the commencement of Employee's duties allowed by and with Employer and the compensation paid, Employee and Employer willfully enter into this Agreement.

3. Role and Responsibilities: In this section clearly define an employee's role within the company such as official title. Also include the employee's primary duties and responsibilities. It is always good to include a statement that "roles and responsibilities are subject to change" even if you are not sure they will. This will give you room to grow as an organization, and move people as your needs change.

4. Compensation: Include all salary details including pay structure (lump sum, weekly, bi-weekly, etc.) wage (an annual, hourly, or daily amount), or commission (based on work output).

5. Benefits: If you are offering benefits, include them here. <u>Benefits include such things as insurance plans and premiums paid on your employees behalf or 401K matching. Also include paid annual or sick leave and the rate of accrual. Don't forget to include special benefits like performance-based perks, sport/event passes, or any other benefit you choose.</u>

6. Confidential Information

In the performance of Employee's job duties with Employer, Employee will be exposed to Employer's Confidential Information. "Confidential Information" means information or material that is commercially valuable to Employer and not generally known in the industry. Employee shall keep Confidential Information, whether or not prepared or developed by Employee, in the strictest confidence. Employee will not disclose such secrets to anyone outside Employer without Employer's prior written consent. Nor will Employee make use of any Confidential Information for Employee's own purposes or the benefit of anyone other than Employer.

However, Employee shall have no obligation to treat as confidential any information which: (a) was in Employee's possession or known by Employee, without an obligation to keep it confidential, before such information was disclosed to Employee by Employer; (b) is or becomes public knowledge through a source other than Employee and through no fault of Employee; or (c) is or becomes lawfully available to Employee from a source other than Employer.

7. Noncompetition *(A non-compete agreement is a clause or contract that adds limitations to the employment contract. These agreements protect the business by restricting the other party from performing similar work for a specific period of time, within a certain geographical area.)* To protect the Confidential Information while Employee is employed by Employer, and for **(state restrictive time period in years)** post-employment period thereafter, Employee shall not:

•   plan for, acquire any financial interest in, or perform services for (as an independent Employee, employee, consultant, officer, director, principal, agent or otherwise) any business that would require Employee to use or disclose any Confidential Information; or

•   perform services (as an independent Employee, employee, consultant, officer, director, principal, agent or otherwise) that are similar to Employee's current duties or responsibilities for any person or entity that, during the term of this Agreement, engages in any business activity in which Employer is then engaged or proposes to be engaged and that conducts its business in the following territory: **(Include restricted region: state, region, country)**.

#Tip: A non-compete agreement cannot last indefinitely, and cannot restrict employees in every geographical area. It is common that such agreements last 1-2 years, and in the geographical area of the primary business transactions (state, region, country, etc.) Regions can be worldwide in cases where your transactions reach a worldwide audience, for example Internet based business may have a worldwide audience.

8. Nondisclosure

Receiving Party shall hold and maintain the Confidential Information in the strictest confidence for the sole and exclusive benefit of the Disclosing Party.

- Receiving Party shall carefully restrict access to Confidential Information to employees, Employees and third parties as is reasonably required and shall require those persons to sign nondisclosure restrictions at least as protective as those in this Agreement.

- Receiving Party shall not, without prior written approval of Disclosing Party, use for Receiving Party's own benefit either for private or commercial use, publish, copy, or otherwise disclose to others, or permit the use by others for their benefit or to the detriment of Disclosing Party, any Confidential Information including but not limited to trade secrets, business plans and financial records.

- Receiving Party shall return to Disclosing Party any and all records, notes, and other written, printed, or tangible materials in its possession pertaining to Confidential Information immediately if Disclosing Party requests it in writing.

9. Non-Solicitation (A *non-solicitation* agreement is a clause or contract in which an employee agrees not to solicit a company's clients or customers, for his or her own benefit or for the benefit of another person or company)

While Employee is employed by Employer, and for post-employment non-solicitation period for

(State period of non-solicitation in years. This should match the non-compete duration) thereafter, Employee shall not:

- employ, attempt to employ, or solicit for employment by any other person or entity, any Employer Employees;

- encourage any consultant, independent contractor, employee or any other person or entity to end their relationship or stop doing business with Employer, or help any person or entity do so or attempt to do so;

- solicit or attempt to solicit or obtain business or trade from any of Employer's current or prospective customers or clients or help any person or entity do so or attempt to do so; or

- obtain or attempt to obtain any Confidential Information for any purpose whatsoever except as required by Employer to enable Employee to perform his or her job duties.

10. Right to an Injunction *(Injunction: An injunction is a judicial order that restrains a person from beginning or continuing an action threatening or invading the legal right of another.)*

A breach or threatened breach of this Agreement may result in irreparable harm such that money damages would be an inadequate remedy and extremely difficult to measure. In addition, the Employer shall be entitled to an injunction to restrain Employee from such breach or threatened breach. Nothing in this Agreement shall be construed as preventing Employer from pursuing any remedy at law or equity for any breach or threatened breach.

11. Survivability

This Agreement will survive the termination, for any reason, of Employee's employment with Employer.

12. Entire Agreement

This is the entire agreement between the parties. It replaces and supersedes any and all oral agreements between the parties, as well as any prior writings. This Agreement may not be amended except in a writing signed by both parties.

13. Successors and Assignees

This agreement binds and benefits the heirs, successors, and assignees of the parties.

14. Waiver

The failure to exercise any right provided in this Agreement shall not be a waiver of prior or subsequent rights.

15. Governing Law

This agreement will be governed by and construed in accordance with the laws of the **(State of legal authority)**.

16. Severability

If any court determines that any provision of this agreement is invalid or unenforceable, any invalidity or unenforceability will affect only that provision and will not make any other provision of this agreement invalid or unenforceable and shall be modified, amended, or limited only to the extent necessary to render it valid and enforceable.

Employee has carefully read and considered all clauses of this Agreement and agrees that all of the restrictions set forth are fair and reasonably required to protect Employer's interests.

Employee has received a copy of this Agreement as signed by both parties.

[Signature and date omitted]

#Tip: An employment agreement can be used for any type of employee including full-time, part-time, and contractors.

As you can see, an employment agreement is vital to any business. Ensuring your employees are aware of all the benefits of employment with your company, and all restrictions, gives you added protection against legal claims.

Quiz 3

1. You have created an employment agreement for the first time and decide to include a non-compete clause. What is the most appropriate duration of validity?

   a. Two years or less

   b. Indefinitely

   c. More information is needed

2. In the same employment agreement your non-compete clause covers all of the necessary terms except for the restrictive region. What do you include in the restrictive region area?

   a. The city, state, or country

   b. Worldwide in all circumstances

   c. More information is needed

3. You decide to hire Victor as the new Director of Technical Support. You draft his employment agreement and include his wages, benefits, and responsibilities in precise detail. You also include his period of employment stating that it will no less than five years. Everything is working out great until one year later when your business needs change, and you ask Victor to take on additional duties. He refuses to perform additional duties and points to his employment agreement. Because you described his responsibilities in detail you are stuck with him and now have to hire another staff member, who is not in the budget. What would have been the best thing to do to protect yourself prior to Victor's employment?

a. Describe roles and responsibilities in broad terms that may cover additional duties

b. Include a statement indicating that responsibilities are subject to change

c. Not include a section for responsibilities

d. Both a and b

e. All of the above

Closing

The three contracts presented in this workbook were chosen, because they offer a wide range of legal terms and language that will help you familiarize yourself with other legal agreements. Don't be overwhelmed at the amount of material and unfamiliar terms. It takes time and practice to gain a solid understanding of any legal language. The beauty of understanding contract language is that, once you understand it, you can apply your knowledge to drafting and reviewing your own personal and business related contracts. Properly reviewing your own contracts, at least some of them can save you hundreds if not thousands of dollars.

It is a fact that we will all, at some point in our lives, agree to something whether it be orally or in writing. The agreements we make, will either be empty promises or binding contracts. When what you promise or someone promises you, becomes legally binding, make sure you are getting what you bargained for.

Disclaimer: We Love Lawyers!

Key Terms

Abate: to make or become less in amount, intensity, degree, etc.

Acceptance: the action of consenting to receive or undertake something offered.

Binding: (of an agreement or promise) involving an obligation that cannot be broken.

Capital: wealth in the form of money or other assets owned by a person or organization or available or contributed for a particular purpose such as starting a company or investing.

Clause: a section, phrase, paragraph, or segment of a legal document, such as a contract, deed, will, or constitution, that relates to a particular point.

Consideration: anything of value promised to another when making a contract.

Entity: a thing with distinct and independent existence.

Land: real property, real estate (and all that grows thereon), and the right to minerals underneath and the airspace over it.

Lease: a contractual arrangement calling for the lessee (user) to pay the lessor (owner) for use of an asset.

Offer: the act of giving someone the opportunity to accept something.

Party: a person or group of persons that compose a single entity which can be identified as one for the purposes of the law.

Power of Attorney: a document that allows you to appoint a person or organization to handle your affairs while you're unavailable or unable to do so.

Real Property: property that is attached directly to land, as well as the land itself.

Subrogation: the right for an insurer to pursue a third party that caused an insurance loss to the insured.

Time is of the Essence: indicates that the parties to an agreement must perform by the time to which the parties have agreed if a delay will cause material harm.

Answer Key

Quiz 1 - Answers: b, a, c

Quiz 2 - Answers: a, d, b

Quiz 3 - Answers: a, c, d

References

Farlex, Inc. (2003-2015). *Dictionary/Thesaurus*. Retrieved 2015, from The Free Dictionary by Farlex.

Farnsworth, E. A., Young, W. F., Sanger, C., Cohen, N. B., & Brooks, R. R. (2008). *Contracts Cases And Materials* (Seventh ed.). New York, NY: Thompson Reuter/ Foundation Press.

Merriam-Webster, Inc. (2015). *Merriam-Webster*. Retrieved 2015, from Merriam-Webster Online Dictionary: http://i.word.com

Thomson West. (2014). *Black's Law Dictionary* (Tenth ed.). Secaucus, NJ: Thomson West.

The Childress Group, LLC